Contents

Any words appearing in the text in bold, **like this**, are explained in the Glossary.

What is a wheel?

A machine is a man-made **device**. All machines make our lives easier by helping us to do jobs. This simple machine is called a wheel.

Very useful machines

Wheels

Chris Oxlade

Heinemann
LIBRARY

H www.heinemann.co.uk/library

Visit our website to find out more information about Heinemann Library books.

To order:

☎ Phone 44 (0) 1865 888066

▤ Send a fax to 44 (0) 1865 314091

▢ Visit the Heinemann Bookshop at www.heinemann.co.uk/library to browse our catalogue and order online.

First published in Great Britain by Heinemann Library, Halley Court, Jordan Hill, Oxford OX2 8EJ, part of Harcourt Education.
Heinemann is a registered trademark of Harcourt Education Ltd.

Editorial: Nicole Irving and Georga Godwin
Design: Richard Parker and AMR
Picture Research: Rebecca Sodergren and Pete Morris
Production: Séverine Ribierre

Originated by Ambassador Litho Ltd
Printed and bound in China by South China Printing Company

ISBN 0 431 17895 X (hardback)
07 06 05 04 03
10 9 8 7 6 5 4 3 2 1

ISBN 0 431 17901 8 (paperback)
08 07 06 05 04
10 9 8 7 6 5 4 3 2 1

British Library Cataloguing in Publication Data

Oxlade, Chris
Wheels – Very Useful Machines
621.8'2
A full catalogue record for this book is available from the British Library.

Acknowledgements

The publishers would like to thank the following for permission to reproduce photographs: Alamy Images **pp. 6**, **21**, **22**, **27**; Comstock Images **p. 5**; Corbis/David H. Wells **p. 10**; Corbis/Duomo **p. 16**; Corbis/James A. Sugar **p. 18**; Corbis/Jens Haas **p. 8**; Corbis/Lester Lefkowitz **p. 29**; Corbis/Robert Estall **p. 26**; Corbis/Royalty-Free **p. 24**; DK Images **p. 4**; Getty Images **pp. 19**, **20**; Giles Chapman **p. 17**; Imagebank **pp. 12**, **25**; Peter Morris **pp. 7**, **9**, **11**; Pictor Uniphoto **p. 15**; SPL **p. 14**; Taxi/Robert Clare **p. 13**; Trip/J. Greenburg **p. 23**.

Cover photograph of aeroplane wheel is reproduced with permission of Imagebank.

Every effort has been made to contact copyright holders of any material reproduced in this book. Any omissions will be rectified in subsequent printings if notice is given to the publishers.

A wheel is a very
useful machine.
This pushchair
has three wheels.
The wheels make
it easy to move
the pushchair
forwards and
backwards.

What does a wheel do?

Most wheels you see are on cars, bicycles and other things that move along, like roller blades and pushchairs. The wheels make it easier for these things to move.

Wheels also make **pushes** and **pulls** bigger or smaller. This wheel on a hi-fi machine is on a **rod**. A small push on the wheel makes a large push that turns the rod.

Parts of a wheel

spokes

A wheel is a round, flat object. Solid wheels are made from one piece of material. Some wheels have holes in them and **spokes** to make them lighter.

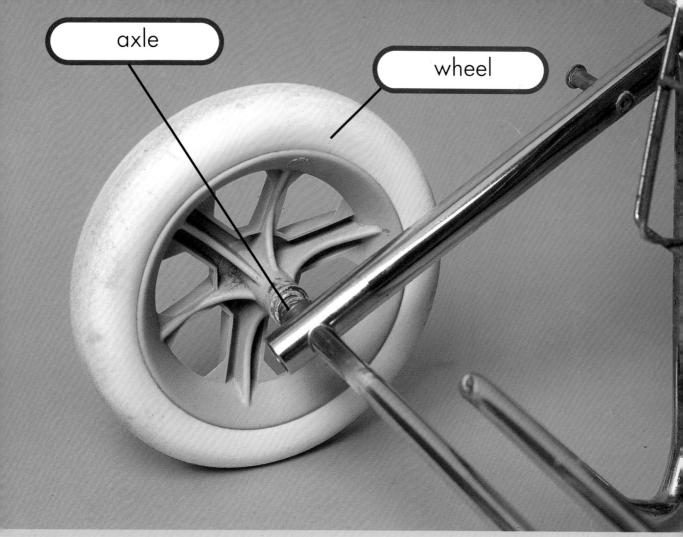

axle

wheel

The centre of a wheel is always
connected to a **rod** called an **axle**.
Sometimes the axle turns round with the
wheel. Sometimes the wheel spins and
the axle stays still.

How a wheel works

Heavy things are hard to push along the ground because of a **force** called **friction**. Friction stops them moving easily. Wheels make friction much smaller.

Wheels can also make **pushes** and **pulls** bigger or smaller. A large doorknob works like a wheel. A small push to turn the doorknob makes a big push on the door **latch**.

Wheels for moving

Wheels let things move along easily and smoothly. A skateboard has four tough rubber wheels. The wheels press on the ground and spin round as the skateboard moves.

Most wheelchairs have two big wheels
at the back and two small wheels at the
front. The person in the chair **pushes**
on the rims of the big wheels to make
the chair move.

Wheels for transport

Motorcycles, cars, buses and trucks all have wheels. The wheels let these heavy **vehicles** roll smoothly along the road. **Rubber** tyres help give a smooth ride and stop the wheels slipping about.

Train wheels run on metal tracks. They do not need tyres. The two wheels on opposite sides of the train are joined by an **axle**. Because they need to be very strong, the wheels are made from solid steel.

Making wheels turn

Wheels also make **vehicles** move. Pressing on the pedals of this tricycle makes the front wheel turn. The wheel **pushes** against the path. This makes the tricycle go forwards.

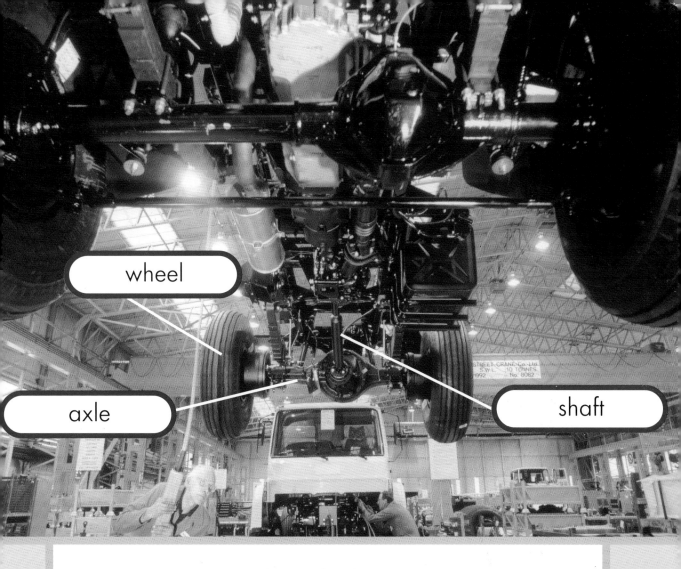

wheel

axle

shaft

Cars, buses and trucks have engines. This truck's engine turns a **rod** called a shaft. The shaft turns the back wheels. The wheels push against the road. This makes the truck move.

Wheels for rolling

Some wheels do not move along. They just spin round instead, like this rolling pin. It rolls along the pastry when you **push** it, flattening the dough.

This parcel is being pushed along a roller table. The top of the table has lots of wheels. The wheels spin under the parcel, letting it slide along easily.

More useful wheels

A wheel and **rod** together makes turning things easier. A truck is steered by turning a rod attached to the wheels. The large steering wheel makes it easy to turn the rod.

Here is a wheel for turning a tap on and off. Turning the wheel turns a rod that goes into the tap. Turning the rod without the wheel would be very hard.

tap

Wheels in machines

Many complicated machines have wheels that help them to work. This crane has lots of **pulley** wheels that help it to lift heavy loads.

This machine is for measuring distances. The person pushes the machine along. This makes the wheel turn. Each time the wheel turns once, it means the person has walked one metre.

Gear wheels

A **gear wheel** is a special sort of wheel. It has teeth all the way round its edge. Hundreds of different machines have gear wheels inside.

Gear wheels are always used together.
They are put next to each other so that
their teeth meet up. When one wheel turns,
the teeth make the other wheel turn, too.

Gear wheels in machines

Many machines have **gear wheels** inside that help them to work. These huge gear wheels work the moving parts in a wind mill. They help to grind wheat and other grains.

Some gears wheels are very tiny. These gear wheels are inside a wristwatch. They make the hour hand and minute hand turn at the right speed.

Amazing wheel facts

- The wheel is one of the oldest machines in the world. It was invented more than 5000 years ago.
- On old sailing ships the heavy anchor was pulled up from the seabed by a huge wheel called a capstan wheel.
- Before wheels were invented, people moved heavy stones using logs for rollers.
- The tiniest **gear wheels** ever made are not as wide as a hair from your head. They were made to see just how small we could make them.

- The monster wheels of the Terex Titan dumper truck are much taller than a person.

Glossary

axle rod that connects to the centre of a wheel. Sometimes an axle turns with a wheel. Sometimes the wheel spins around the axle.

device thing that does a job. A clothes peg is a device. So is an electronic calculator.

force energy that pushes or pulls something

friction force that tries to slow down moving objects

gear wheel wheel with teeth around its edge

latch device that stops a door opening

pull to hold something and move it closer. To pull towards yourself.

pulley — simple machine that makes lifting or pulling objects easier

push — to press on something and move it away. To push away from yourself.

rod — long, thin piece of metal

rubber — material that tyres are made of. Rubber is tough but bendy and grips the road well.

shaft — rod that spins around

spoke — rod that connects the centre of a wheel to the outside of a wheel. A wheel with spokes is lighter than a solid wheel.

vehicle — machine that carries passengers or cargo from place to place

More books to read

Wheels and Cranks, Angela Royston (Heinemann Library: 2000)

What do Wheels and Cranks do?, David Glover (Heinemann Library: 1996)

Wheels and Axles, Michael Dahl (Franklin Watts, 2001)

Toybox Science: Gears, Chris Ollerenshaw and Pat Triggs (A and C Black: 2001)

Index